Sa... ...
for Every Day

Heather,
Continue to keep &
to spread the faith.
Prayerful best wishes,
Fr. Mike Kerrigan, CSP
08/05/08

OTHER BOOKS IN THE SERIES

The Little Way for Every Day:
Thoughts from Thérèse of Lisieux
by St. Thérèse of Lisieux;
selected and translated by
Francis Broome, CSP

Saint Teresa of Avila for Every Day:
Reflections from The Interior Castle
edited by Kieran Kavanaugh, OCD

Saint John of the Cross for Every Day
edited by Kieran Kavanaugh, OCD

Scripture Verses for Every Day
edited by Amgad Maher Salama

Saint Paul the Apostle for Every Day

*A Vision That Inspires,
A Mission for Life*

Michael P. Kerrigan, CSP

Paulist Press
New York/Mahwah, NJ

The Scripture quotations contained herein are from the New Revised Standard Version: Catholic Edition, copyright © 1989 and 1993 by the Division of Christian Education of the National Council of the Churches of Christ in the United States of America. Used by permission. All rights reserved.

Cover design by Sharyn Banks
Book design by Lynn Else
The photographs in this book are by the author.

Copyright © 2008 by Paulist Press, Inc.

All rights reserved. No part of this book may be reproduced or transmitted in any form or by any means, electronic or mechanical, including photocopying, recording, or by any information storage and retrieval system without permission in writing from the Publisher.

Library of Congress Cataloging-in-Publication Data

Kerrigan, Michael P.
  Saint Paul the Apostle for every day : a vision that inspires, a mission for life / Michael P. Kerrigan.
    p. cm. — (Every day ; 6)
  ISBN-13: 978-0-8091-4567-6 (alk. paper)
  1. Bible. N.T. Epistles of Paul—Theology. 2. Bible. N.T. Epistles of Paul—Quotations. 3. Devotional calendars. I. Title.
  BS2651.K46 2008
  242'.2—dc22
                                                            2008019284

Published by Paulist Press
997 Macarthur Boulevard
Mahwah, New Jersey 07430

www.paulistpress.com

Printed and bound in the
United States of America

Contents

Map: World of St. Paul vii
Introduction ix

January
   Coming to Know God: Week of Prayer
   for Christian Unity (January 18–25) 1

February
   God's Love for Us: The Love of Christ
   Impels Us 11

March
   The Call to Repentance and Ongoing
   Conversion: The Law of Christ
   Sets Us Free 19

April
   New Life in Christ: God's Plan of
   Salvation 29

May
   The Holy Spirit Guides Us:
   Life in the Spirit 37

June
    The Body of Christ: Truly Becoming
    What We Eat and Drink 45

July
    Life in Community: Seeking Ways of
    Organizing the Practical Christian Life . .55

August
    The Gospel Message Requires Persistent
    Preaching: The Value in Writing
    Letters 63

September
    Exhortations and Positive Thoughts for
    Christian Living 73

October
    The Ongoing Mission of Evangelization:
    Proclaiming the Good News Continues . .81

November
    The Hope of the Resurrection:
    The Promise of Eternal Life 91

December
    Recalling the First Coming of Jesus in
    History: Preparing for Christ's Return
    in Majesty 101

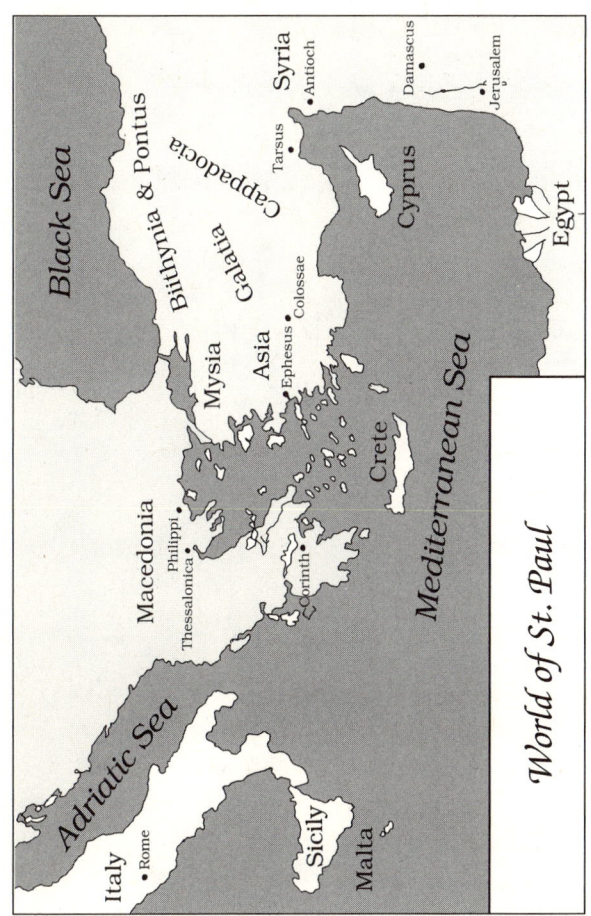

Introduction

The announcement made by Pope Benedict XVI on June 28, 2007, during the vespers service at the Basilica of St. Paul Outside-the-Walls in Rome, for a Special Jubilee Year to the Apostle Paul (June 28, 2008, to June 29, 2009) prompted the compilation of this short work as another title in the Paulist Press "…for Every Day" series.

On the occasion in which the bimillennium of this important figure's birth is being celebrated, this jubilee offers a unique and special opportunity to recall the life, example, spirituality, and lasting legacy of one Christianity's most important and influential leaders.

Saint Paul the Apostle may be best described as an intriguing individual who was inspired by both "a vision and a mission in life." His life was profoundly affected one day by a dramatic conversion experience on the road to Damascus that not only impacted him personally but many others as well. Proud of

Mural, Church of St. Paul the Apostle, New York

his background as a Greek-speaking Jew and a Roman citizen from Tarsus, this man was chosen to become a special instrument in bringing the gospel message to the Gentiles of the Mediterranean world in the first century AD.

An influential missionary preacher, a prolific author whose writings have perdured throughout the many centuries and are still read and studied, and an innovator who sought to communicate with others by using the available means and modes of his day, Paul of Tarsus found various ways to bring the gospel message to new people in the different locales of his day. Although his message was addressed primarily to communities throughout the eastern parts of the Roman Empire in Greece and Asia Minor that he helped establish, his theological reflections, insights, and practical advice still resonate today.

This short book tries to capture the thoughts of Saint Paul the Apostle in the context of a calendar year. Although the best way to study and appreciate Saint Paul is by reading his letters in the New Testament and studying them in the context and historical setting in which they were written, this approach attempts to use major Pauline themes by organizing them into months. Each month offers a theme accompanied by reflections and a different daily scripture verse taken from the various letters of Saint Paul and words attributed to him from stories narrated in the Acts of the Apostles. In addition, the various feasts and celebrations in the Church's liturgical calendar for that month are noted.

For the reader already familiar with Saint Paul, these daily verses may appear isolated and out of context from his entire letter, but they encapsulate a significant thought for the day. For the reader not familiar with Saint Paul, hopefully these daily verses will encourage you to read his letters in the context in which they were written and that you will come to a greater appreciation of Pauline theology and spirituality.

The suggestion is to use this guide for daily reading, reflection, and inspiration. Each day as you read the particular scripture verse from Saint Paul, recall the vision and mission of this great apostle. Realize the power of his words, their significance, how these words challenge the present age along with ways in which you can apply them to your own life.

May this be an opportunity to follow in the footsteps of Saint Paul, to come to know the thoughts and insights of this timeless teacher of the Christian faith and to continue his vision and mission every day as twenty-first century followers of the Lord Jesus Christ.

January

Coming to Know God: Week of Prayer for Christian Unity (January 18–25)

Becoming more aware, attentive, and appreciative of God's presence in our daily lives is a resolution that individuals often make at the beginning of a new calendar year. The nativity celebration recalls vividly God's manifestation into human history in the person of Jesus in order that we might come to know, love, and serve God better in our personal lives.

The annual Week of Prayer for Christian Unity is a reminder about the sad consequences

Exterior, Basilica of Saint Peter, Rome

of human history in which various misunderstandings and theological differences have often divided Christians rather than united them in Jesus Christ. It is a good opportunity to pray for those involved in ecumenism and the work of Christian unity so that "all may be may one" as Jesus desires for all Christian members in the body of Christ.

1
The Blessed Virgin Mary, Mother of God

Paul, a servant of God and an apostle of Jesus Christ, for the sake of the faith of God's elect and the knowledge of truth that is in accordance with godliness, in the hope of eternal life that God, who never lies, promised before the ages began—in due time he revealed his word through the proclamation with which I have been entrusted by the command of God our Savior. (Titus 1:1–3)

2
Saints Basil the Great and Gregory Nazianzen

Grace to you and peace from God our Father and the Lord Jesus Christ. (2 Cor 1:2)

3

"For who has known the mind of the Lord? Or who has been his counselor? Or who has been given a gift to him, to receive a gift in return?" (Rom 11:34–35)

4

Saint Elizabeth Ann Seton

"The God who made the world and everything in it, he who is Lord of heaven and earth, does not live in shrines made by human hands, nor is he served by human hands, as though he needed anything, since he himself gives to all mortals life and breath and all things." (Acts 17:24–25)

5

Saint John Neumann

I pray that the God of our Lord Jesus Christ, the Father of glory, may give you a spirit of wisdom and revelation as you come to know him. (Eph 1:17)

6

The Epiphany of the Lord

God is faithful; by him you were called into the fellowship of his Son, Jesus Christ our Lord. (1 Cor 1:9)

7

"In past generations, he [God] allowed all the nations to follow their own ways; yet he has not left himself without a witness in doing good—giving you rains from heaven and fruitful seasons, and filling you with food and your hearts with joy." (Acts 14:16–17)

8

But we have this treasure in clay jars, so that it may be made clear that this extraordinary power belongs to God and does not come from us. (2 Cor 4:7)

9

For I am not ashamed of the gospel; it is the power of God for salvation to everyone who has faith... (Rom 1:16)

10

"From one ancestor he [God] made all nations to inhabit the whole earth, and he allotted the times of their existence and the boundaries of the places where they would live, so that they would search for God and perhaps grope for him and find him—though indeed he is not far from each one of us." (Acts 17:26–27)

11
Because you are children, God has sent the Spirit of the Son into our hearts, crying, "Abba! Father!" So you are no longer a slave but a child and if a child then also an heir, through God. (Gal 4:6–7)

12
"I will be your father, and you shall be my sons and daughters, says the Lord Almighty." (2 Cor 6:18)

13
The gifts and the calling of God are irrevocable. (Rom 11:29)

14
"Since we are God's offspring, we ought not to think that the deity is like gold, or silver, or stone, an image formed by the art and imagination of mortals." (Acts 17:29)

15
With all wisdom and insight, he has made known to us the mystery of his will, according to his good pleasure that he set forth in Christ, as a plan for the fullness of time, to gather up all things in him, things in heaven and things on earth. (Eph 1:8–10)

16
If God is for us, who is against us? (Rom 8:31)

17
Saint Anthony

For it is the God who said, "Let light shine out of darkness," who has shone in our hearts to give the light of the knowledge of the glory of God in the face of Jesus Christ. (2 Cor 4:6)

18
Week of Prayer for Christian Unity: January 18–25

Let the peace of Christ rule in your hearts, to which indeed you were called in the one body… (Col 3:15)

19
Now I appeal to you, brothers and sisters, by the name of our Lord Jesus Christ, that all of you be in agreement and that there be no divisions among you, but that you be united in the same mind and the same purpose. (1 Cor 1:10)

20
There is one body and one Spirit, just as you were called to the one hope of your calling, one Lord, one faith, one baptism, one God and

Father of all, who is above all and through all and in all. (Eph 4:4–6)

21
Saint Agnes

For just as the body is one and has many members, and all the members of the body, though many, are one body, so it is with Christ. (1 Cor 12:12)

22

So then, whenever we have an opportunity, let us work for the good of all, and especially for those of the family of faith. (Gal 6:10)

23

You belong to Christ, and Christ belongs to God. (1 Cor 3:23)

24
Saint Francis de Sales

We are ambassadors for Christ, since God is making his appeal through us; we entreat you on behalf of Christ, be reconciled to God. (2 Cor 5:20)

25
The Conversion of Paul

"...I was traveling to Damascus with the authority and commission of the chief priests, when at midday along the road...I saw a light from heaven, brighter than the sun, shining around me and my companions." (Acts 26:12–13)

26
Saints Timothy and Titus

"I asked, 'What am I to do, Lord?'" (Acts 22:10)

27

"The Lord answered....'Get up and stand on your feet; for I have appeared to you for this purpose, to appoint you to serve and testify to the things in which you have seen me.'" (Acts 26:15–16)

28
Saint Thomas Aquinas

O the depth of the riches and wisdom and knowledge of God! How unsearchable are his judgments and how inscrutable his ways! (Rom 11:33)

29
For we do not proclaim ourselves; we proclaim Jesus Christ as Lord and ourselves as your slaves for Jesus' sake. (2 Cor 4:5)

30
"We bring you the good news that what God promised to our ancestors he has fulfilled for us..." (Acts 13:32–33)

31
Saint John Bosco

...If I were still pleasing people, I would not be a servant of Christ. (Gal 1:10)

February

God's Love for Us: The Love of Christ Impels Us

Pope Benedict XVI's first encyclical, *Deus Caritas Est*, promulgated on January 25, 2006, the Feast of the Conversion of Paul the Apostle, is a profound reflection upon the meaning and significance of "God is love."

The word *love* is often used in many ways and has various meanings. Rediscovering the power and significance of God's love is the core message of Christianity.

Saint Paul invites and encourages reflection upon love, not only God's love for us but also the practical ways to live and reflect God's love in our own lives.

Exterior, Basilica of Saint Paul Outside-the-Walls, Rome

1

Blessed be the God and Father of our Lord Jesus Christ, who has blessed us in Christ with every spiritual blessing in the heavenly places, just as he chose us in Christ before the foundation of the world to be holy and blameless before him in love. (Eph 1:3–4)

2

The Presentation of the Lord

"...This is the Messiah, Jesus whom I am proclaiming to you." (Acts 17:3)

3

Saint Blase

For the whole law is summed up in a single commandment, "You shall love your neighbor as yourself." (Gal 5:14)

4

Now concerning love of the brothers and sisters, you do not need to have anyone write to you, for you yourselves have been taught by God to love one another. (1 Thess 4:9)

5
Saint Agatha

May the Lord direct your hearts to the love of God and to the steadfastness of Christ. (2 Thess 3:5)

6
Saint Paul Miki and Companions

I pray that, according to the riches of his glory, he may grant that you may be strengthened in your inner being with power through his Spirit and that Christ may dwell in your hearts through faith, as you are being rooted and grounded in love. (Eph 3:16–17)

7

God proves his love for us in that while we still were sinners Christ died for us. (Rom 5:8)

8

...I received mercy because I had acted ignorantly in unbelief, and the grace of our Lord overflowed for me with the faith and love that are in Christ Jesus. (1 Tim 1:13–14)

9

We know that all things work together for good for those who love God, who are called according to his purpose. (Rom 8:28)

10
Saint Scholastica

Grace be with all who have an undying love for our Lord Jesus Christ. (Eph 6:24)

11
Our Lady of Lourdes

…Pursue righteousness, faith, love, and peace, along with those who call on the Lord from a pure heart. (2 Tim 2:22)

12

Speaking the truth in love, we must grow up in every way into him who is the head, into Christ. (Eph 4:15)

13

May our Lord Jesus Christ himself and God our Father, who loved us and through grace gave us eternal comfort and good hope, comfort your hearts and strengthen them in every good work and word. (2 Thess 2:16–17)

14
Saints Cyril and Methodius

Love is patient; love is kind; love is not envious or boastful or arrogant or rude… (1 Cor 13:4–5)

15

Peace be to the whole community, and love with faith, from God the Father and the Lord Jesus Christ. (Eph 6:23)

16

We must always give thanks to God for you, brothers and sisters, as is right, because your faith is growing abundantly, and the love of everyone of you for one another is increasing. (2 Thess 1:3)

17

Let love be genuine; hate what is evil, hold fast to what is good; love one another with mutual affection; outdo one another in showing honor. (Rom 12:9–10)

18

We always give thanks to God for all of you and mention you in our prayers, constantly remembering before our God and Father your work of faith and labor of love and steadfastness of hope in our Lord Jesus Christ. (1 Thess 1:2–3)

19

So I urge you to reaffirm your love for him. (2 Cor 2:8)

20

As God's chosen ones, holy and beloved, clothe yourselves with compassion, kindness, humility, meekness, and patience. (Col 3:12)

21

Who will separate us from the love of Christ? Will hardship, or distress, or persecution, or famine, or nakedness, or peril, or sword? (Rom 8:35)

22

The Chair of Saint Peter

Be imitators of God, as beloved children, and live in love, as Christ loved us and gave himself up for us... (Eph 5:1–2)

23
Saint Polycarp

Owe no one anything, except to love one another; for the one who loves another has fulfilled the law. (Rom 13:8)

24

May the Lord make you increase and abound in love for one another and for all, just as we abound in love for you. (1 Thess 3:12)

25

Clothe yourselves with love, which binds everything together in perfect harmony. (Col 3:14)

26

Faith, hope, and love abide, these three; and the greatest of these is love. (1 Cor 13:13)

27

For the love of Christ urges us on... (2 Cor 5:14)

28

Let all that you do be done in love. (1 Cor 16:14)

29

Grace to you and peace from God our Father and the Lord Jesus Christ. (1 Cor 1:3)

March

The Call to Repentance and Ongoing Conversion: The Law of Christ Sets Us Free

Saint Paul underwent a dramatic conversion experience on the road to Damascus that had a tremendous impact upon him. Although this life-changing event happened in a specific and identifiable incident in his life, Saint Paul's conversion serves as a model and an example for the Christian life. Rather than primarily understanding conversion as a single, isolated moment in the past, conversion should be viewed as an

The Incarceration of Saints Peter and Paul,
Mamertime Prison, Rome

ongoing, lifelong process in relationship with God and others.

The seasonal theme of Lent is the call to repentance, conversion, and the need to reform our lives. Admitting the need to change some aspect of our lives, seeking God's help, and having the courage and resolve to become better Christians are important aspects of this ongoing call to conversion and repentance.

Christ's law of love should not be viewed as an imposition from an outside authority with a fear of punitive measures, but as an experience that is freeing, transformative, and liberates us from sin.

1
"Who are you, Lord?" (Acts 9:5)

2
Ever since the creation of the world his eternal power and divine nature, invisible though they are, have been understood and seen through the things he [God] has made... (Rom 1:20)

3
For we are what he has made us, created in Christ Jesus for good works, which God prepared beforehand to be our way of life. (Eph 2:10)

4

One night the Lord said to Paul in a vision, "Do not be afraid, but speak and do not be silent; for I am with you, and no one will lay a hand on you to harm you..." (Acts 18:9–10)

5

...Do you not realize that God's kindness is meant to lead you to repentance? (Rom 2:4)

6

While God has overlooked the times of human ignorance, now he commands all people everywhere to repent. (Acts 17:30)

7

Saints Perpetua and Felicity

I am grateful to Christ Jesus our Lord, who has strengthened me, because he judged me faithful and appointed me to his service, even though I was formerly a blasphemer, a persecutor, and a man of violence... (1 Tim 1:12–13)

8

...The righteousness of God has been disclosed, and is attested by the law and the prophets, the righteousness of God through faith in Jesus Christ for all who believe... (Rom 3:21–22)

9

"Beware, therefore, that what the prophets said does not happen to you: 'Look, you scoffers! Be amazed and perish, for in your days I am doing a work, a work that you will never believe, even if someone tells you.'" (Acts 13:40–41)

10

…We have come to believe in Christ Jesus, so that we might be justified by faith in Christ, and not by doing the works of the law, because no one will be justified by the works of the law. (Gal 2:16)

11

"I am a Jew, born in Tarsus in Cilicia, but brought up in this city at the feet of Gamaliel, educated strictly according to our ancestral law, being zealous for God, just as all of you are today. I persecuted this Way up to the point of death by binding both men and women and putting them in prison." (Acts 22:3–4)

12

For by grace you have been saved through faith, and this is not your own doing; it is the gift of God—not the result of works, so that no one may boast. (Eph 2:8–9)

13

For we hold that a person is justified by faith apart from works prescribed by the law. (Rom 3:28)

14

The law was our disciplinarian until Christ came, so that we might be justified by faith. (Gal 3:24)

15

For it is not the hearers of the law who are righteous in God's sight, but the doers of the law who will be justified. (Rom 2:13)

16

With the eyes of your heart enlightened, you may know what is the hope to which he has called you, what are the riches of his glorious inheritance among the saints. (Eph 1:18)

17

Saint Patrick

Let the same mind be in you that was in Christ Jesus. (Phil 2:5)

18

If you confess with your lips that Jesus is Lord and believe in your heart that God raised him from the dead, you will be saved. (Rom 10:9)

19

Saint Joseph, Husband of the Blessed Virgin Mary

"...Up to this day I have lived my life with a clear conscience before God." (Acts 23:1)

20

Do not let sin exercise dominion in your mortal bodies, to make you obey their passions. (Rom 6:12)

21

So we do not lose heart. Even though our outer nature is wasting away, our inner nature is being renewed day by day. (2 Cor 4:16)

22

Do not deceive yourselves. If you think that you are wise in this age, you should become fools so that you may become wise. For the wisdom of this world is foolishness with God... (1 Cor 3:18–19)

23

I do not understand my own actions. For I do not do what I want, but I do the very thing I hate. (Rom 7:15)

24

"Bear with one another...forgive each other; just as the Lord has forgiven you, so you also must forgive." (Col 3:13)

25

The Annunciation of the Lord

When the fullness of time had come, God sent his Son, born of a woman, born under the law, in order to redeem those who were under the law, so that we might receive adoption as children. (Gal 4:4–5)

26

For sin will have no dominion over you, since you are not under law but under grace. (Rom 6:14)

27
He [God] has fixed a day on which he will have the world judged in righteousness by a man whom he has appointed, and of this he has given assurance to all by raising him from the dead. (Acts 17:31)

28
For the message about the cross is foolishness to those who are perishing, but to us who are being saved it is the power of God. (1 Cor 1:18)

29
Do not be overcome by evil, but overcome evil with good. (Rom 12:21)

30
For God's foolishness is wiser than human wisdom, and God's weakness is stronger than human strength. (1 Cor 1:25)

31
For to me, living is Christ and dying is gain. (Phil 1:21)

Tarsus Gate, Tarsus, Turkey

April

New Life in Christ: God's Plan of Salvation

The paschal mystery of suffering, dying, and rising to new life applies not only to Jesus, but also is a model and example for all Christians to follow. Saint Paul emphasizes the need to "die to our old selves" in order to have the fullness of life that Jesus Christ offers us. The world of nature helps to illustrate this process: to live in Christ is to be part of a new creation.

Life should be lived not as "a problem to be solved" but rather as "a mystery to be lived." God has invited everyone to be active participants rather than passive spectators in a mysterious plan that unfolds in our lives.

1

…Grace to you and peace from God our Father and the Lord Jesus Christ. (Rom 1:7)

2

"God raised him from the dead; and for many days he appeared to those who came up with him from Galilee to Jerusalem, and they are now his witnesses to the people." (Acts 13:30–31)

3

This is right and is acceptable in the sight of God our Savior, who desires everyone to be saved and to come to the knowledge of the truth. (1 Tim 2:3–4)

4

"Everyone who calls on the name of the Lord shall be saved." (Rom 10:13)

5

"He has also said in another psalm, 'You will not let your Holy One experience corruption.'" (Acts 13:35)

6
God shows no partiality. (Rom 2:11)

7
Saint John Baptist de la Salle

He it is who gave himself for us that he might redeem us from all iniquity and purify for himself a people of his own who are zealous for good deeds. (Titus 2:14)

8
Therefore just as one man's trespass led to condemnation for all, so one man's act of righteousness leads to justification and life for all. (Rom 5:18)

9
For while we live, we are always being given up to death for Jesus' sake, so that the life of Jesus may be made visible in our mortal flesh. (2 Cor 4:11)

10
For just as by the one man's disobedience the many were made sinners, so by the one man's obedience the many will be made righteous. (Rom 5:19)

11
Saint Stanislaus

...If you are confident that you belong to Christ, remind yourself of this, that just as you belong to Christ, so also do we. (2 Cor 10:7)

12

I give thanks to my God always for you because of the grace of God that has been given you in Christ Jesus. (1 Cor 1:4)

13

So if anyone is in Christ, there is a new creation: everything old has passed away; see, everything has become new! (2 Cor 5:17)

14

"I do my best always to have a clear conscience toward God and all people." (Acts 24:16)

15

He will also strengthen you to the end, so that you may be blameless on the day of our Lord Jesus Christ. (1 Cor 1:8)

16

It is God who establishes us with you in Christ and has anointed us, by putting his seal on us and giving us his Spirit in our hearts as a first installment. (2 Cor 1:21–22)

17

Welcome one another, therefore, just as Christ has welcomed you, for the glory of God. (Rom 15:7)

18

He who rescued us from so deadly a peril will continue to rescue us; on him we have set our hope that he will rescue us again. (2 Cor 1:10)

19

Athletes exercise self-control in all things; they do it to receive a perishable wreath, but we an imperishable one. (1 Cor 9:25)

20

For we are the aroma of Christ to God among those who are being saved and among those who are perishing; to the one a fragrance from death to death, to the other a fragrance from life to life… (2 Cor 2:15–16)

21
It is no longer I who live, but it is Christ who lives in me… (Gal 2:20)

22
Such is the confidence that we have through Christ toward God. (2 Cor 3:4)

23
Do you not know that in a race the runners compete, but only one receives the prize? Run in such a way that you may win it. (1 Cor 9:24)

24
Indeed, this is our boast, the testimony of our conscience: we have behaved in the world with frankness and godly sincerity, not by earthly wisdom but by the grace of God… (2 Cor 1:12)

25
Saint Mark

…We also boast in our sufferings, knowing that suffering produces endurance, and endurance produces character, and character produces hope, and hope does not disappoint us… (Rom 5:3–5)

26
So let no one boast about human leaders… (1 Cor 3:21)

27
…We even boast in God through our Lord Jesus Christ, through whom we have now received reconciliation. (Rom 5:11)

28
First of all, then, I urge that supplications, prayers, intercessions, and thanksgivings be made for everyone, for kings and all who are in high positions, so that we may lead a quiet and peaceable life in all godliness and dignity. (1 Tim 2:1–2)

29
Saint Catherine of Siena

…Do I make my plans according to ordinary human standards, ready to say "Yes, yes" and "No, no" at the same time? As surely as God is faithful, our word to you has not been "Yes and No." (2 Cor 1:17–18)

30
I did not shrink from declaring to you the whole purpose of God. (Acts 20:27)

Saint Paul's Well, Tarsus, Turkey

May

The Holy Spirit Guides Us: Life in the Spirit

The Holy Spirit is the animating force both within the life of the individual and the community. Saint Paul repeatedly stresses the importance of being aware of the promptings of the Holy Spirit in our lives. The Holy Spirit strengthens the commitment to Christian discipleship, especially when facing the uncertainties of the present life.

As the animating source that breathed new life upon the early Christian disciples at Pentecost, the Holy Spirit leads us; guides us; challenges us at times to go in new directions, to face difficulties, to endure hardships, and to overcome adversities; and most importantly enables us to trust and have confidence and hope in the future during a transitory human and worldly existence.

1

"Did you receive the Holy Spirit when you became believers?…" (Acts 19:2)

2
Saint Athanasius

When the goodness and loving kindness of God our Savior appeared, he saved us, not because of any works of righteousness that we had done, but according to his mercy, through the water of rebirth and renewal by the Holy Spirit. (Titus 3:4–5)

3
Saints Philip and James

"As a captive to the Spirit, I am on my way to Jerusalem, not knowing what will happen to me there, except that the Holy Spirit testifies to me in every city that imprisonment and persecutions are waiting for me." (Acts 20:22–23)

4

So he came and proclaimed peace to you who were far off and peace to those who were near; for through him both of us have access in one Spirit to the Father. (Eph 2:17–18)

5

For in the one Spirit we were all baptized into body—Jews or Greeks, slaves or free—and we were all made to drink of one Spirit. (1 Cor 12:13)

6

...God's love has been poured into our hearts through the Holy Spirit that has been given to us. (Rom 5:5)

7

This Spirit he poured out on us richly through Jesus Christ our Savior, so that, having been justified by his grace, we might become heirs according to the hope of eternal life. (Titus 3:6–7)

8

For the law of the Spirit of life in Christ Jesus has set you free from the law of sin and of death. (Rom 8:2)

9
Now the Lord is the Spirit, and where the Spirit of the Lord is, there is freedom. (2 Cor 3:17)

10
For freedom Christ has set us free. Stand firm, therefore, and do not submit again to a yoke of slavery. (Gal 5:1)

11
Now we have received not the spirit of the world, but the Spirit that is from God, so that we may understand the gifts bestowed on us by God. (1 Cor 2:12)

12
For those who live according to the flesh set their minds on the things of the flesh, but those who live according to the Spirit set their minds on the things of the Spirit. (Rom 8:5)

13
Our Lady of Fatima

Do you not know that you are God's temple and that God's Spirit dwells in you? (1 Cor 3:16)

14
Saint Matthias

"Keep watch over yourselves and over all the flock, of which the Holy Spirit has made you overseers, to shepherd the church of God..." (Acts 20:28)

15

If we live by the Spirit, let us also be guided by the Spirit. (Gal 5:25)

16

For all who are led by the Spirit of God are children of God. (Rom 8:14)

17

Now there varieties of gifts, but the same Spirit; and there are varieties of services, but the same Lord; and there are varieties of activities, but it is the same God who activates all of them in everyone. (1 Cor 12:4–6)

18

To set the mind on the flesh is death, but to set the mind on the Spirit is life and peace. (Rom 8:6)

19
Not that we are competent of ourselves to claim anything as coming from us; our competence is from God, who has made us competent to be ministers of a new covenant, not of letter but of spirit; for the letter kills, but the Spirit gives life. (2 Cor 3:5–6)

20
...When we cry, "Abba! Father!" it is that very Spirit bearing witness with our spirit that we are children of God. (Rom 8:15–16)

21
He who has prepared us for this very thing is God, who has given us the Spirit as a guarantee. (2 Cor 5:5)

22
To each is given the manifestation of the Spirit for the common good. (1 Cor 12:7)

23
But you are not in the flesh; you are in the Spirit, since the Spirit of God dwells in you. Anyone who does not have the Spirit of Christ does not belong to him. (Rom 8:9)

24

And all of us, with unveiled faces, seeing the glory of the Lord as though reflected in a mirror, are being transformed into the same image from one degree of glory to another; for this comes from the Lord, the Spirit. (2 Cor 3:18)

25

Do not quench the Spirit. (1 Thess 5:19)

26

Saint Philip Neri

The fruit of the Spirit is love, joy, peace, patience, kindness, generosity, faithfulness, gentleness, and self-control. (Gal 5:22–23)

27

Likewise the Spirit helps us in our weakness; for we do not know how to pray as we ought, but that very Spirit intercedes with sighs too deep for words. (Rom 8:26)

28

I am content with weaknesses, insults, hardships, persecutions, and calamities for the sake of Christ; for whenever I am weak, then I am strong. (2 Cor 12:10)

29

For the kingdom of God is not food and drink but righteousness and peace and joy in the Holy Spirit. (Rom 14:17)

30

Pray in the Spirit at all times in every prayer and supplication... (Eph 6:18)

31

The Visitation of the Blessed Virgin Mary

Guard the good treasure entrusted to you, with the help of the Holy Spirit living in us. (2 Tim 1:14)

June

The Body of Christ: Truly Becoming What We Eat and Drink

Saint Paul uses helpful analogies of the physical body and nutrition as ways to offer theological insights and reflections for the Christian life. Just as the body needs care, attention, and proper nourishment in order to grow, develop properly, and attain a healthy existence, the same correlation applies to Christians.

The spiritual sustenance received in the communal eucharistic celebrations needs to become manifest in external actions that are evident to others as well as invigorating the life outside the community. As members of the

Ancient ruins of synagogue, in Antioch of Pisidia, Turkey, where Saints Paul and Barnabas preached (Acts 13:13–52)

body of Christ, it is important that we strive to become what we eat and drink.

1
Saint Justin

He destined us for adoption as his children through Jesus Christ, according to the good pleasure of his will, to the praise of his glorious grace that he freely bestowed on us in the Beloved. (Eph 1:5–6)

2

"As to his raising him from the dead, no more return to corruption, he has spoken in this way, 'I will give you the holy promises made to David.'" (Acts 13:34)

3
Saint Charles Lwanga and Companions

We know that our old self was crucified with him so that the body of sin might be destroyed, and we might no longer be enslaved to sin. (Rom 6:6)

4

"By this Jesus everyone who believes is set free from all those sins from which you could not be freed by the law of Moses." (Acts 13:39)

5
Saint Boniface

You must also consider yourselves dead to sin and alive to God in Christ Jesus. (Rom 6:11)

6

Now you are the body of Christ and individually members of it. (1 Cor 12:27)

7

"For 'In him we live and move and have our being'; as even some of your own poets have said, 'For we too are his offspring.'" (Acts 17:28)

8

For as in one body we have many members, and not all the members have the same function, so we, who are many, are one body in Christ, and individually we are members one of another. (Rom 12:4–5)

9

There is no longer Jew or Greek, there is no longer slave or free, there is no longer male and female; for all of you are one in Christ Jesus. (Gal 3:28)

10

The body does not consist of one member but of many. (1 Cor 12:14)

11

Saint Barnabas

So then you are no longer strangers and aliens, but you are citizens with the saints and also members of the household of God, built upon the foundation of the apostles and prophets, with Christ Jesus himself as the cornerstone. (Eph 2:19–20)

12

For no one can lay any foundation other than the one that has been laid; that foundation is Jesus Christ. (1 Cor 3:11)

13
Saint Anthony of Padua

…We urge you, beloved, to do so more and more, to aspire to live quietly, to mind your own affairs, and to work with your hands, as we directed you, so that you may behave properly toward outsiders and be dependent on no one. (1 Thess 4:10–12)

14

Put away from you all bitterness and wrath and anger and wrangling and slander, together with all malice. (Eph 4:31)

15

Have nothing to do with stupid and senseless controversies; you know that they breed quarrels. (2 Tim 2:23)

16

If one member suffers, all suffer together with it; if one member is honored, all rejoice together with it. (1 Cor 12:26)

17
Be kind to one another, tenderhearted, forgiving one another, as God in Christ has forgiven you. (Eph 4:32)

18
…The bread that we break, is it not a sharing in the body of Christ? (1 Cor 10:16)

19
I appeal to you therefore, brothers and sisters, by the mercies of God, to present your bodies as a living sacrifice, holy and acceptable to God, which is your spiritual worship. (Rom 12:1)

20
Do you not know that your bodies are members of Christ?… (1 Cor 6:15)

21
Saint Aloysius Gonzaga

Stand therefore, and fasten the belt of truth around your waist, and put on the breastplate of righteousness. (Eph 6:14)

22

Because there is one bread, we who are many are one body, for we all partake of the one bread. (1 Cor 10:17)

23

...Who will rescue me from this body of death? Thanks be to God through Jesus Christ our Lord!... (Rom 7:24–25)

24

The Nativity of John the Baptist

Paul said, "John baptized with the baptism of repentance, telling the people to believe in the one who was to come after him, that is, in Jesus." (Acts 19:4)

25

For I am longing to see you so that I may share with you some spiritual gift to strengthen you—or rather so that we may be mutually encouraged by each other's faith, both yours and mine. (Rom 1:11–12)

26

The cup of blessing that we bless, is it not a sharing in the blood of Christ?... (1 Cor 10:16)

27

We have gifts that differ according to the grace given to us: prophecy, in proportion to faith; ministry, in ministering; the teacher, in teaching; the exhorter, in exhortation; the giver, in generosity; the leader, in diligence; the compassionate, in cheerfulness. (Rom 12:6–8)

28

Saint Irenaeus

For as often as you eat this bread and drink the cup, you proclaim the Lord's death until he comes. (1 Cor 11:26)

29

Saints Peter and Paul

For he who worked through Peter making him an apostle to the circumcised also worked through me in sending me to the Gentiles. (Gal 2:8)

30

May the God of steadfastness and encouragement grant you to live in harmony with one another, in accordance with Christ Jesus, so that together you may with one voice glorify the God and Father of our Lord Jesus Christ. (Rom 15:5–6)

Archaeological site, present-day Ephesus, Turkey

July

Life in Community: Seeking Ways of Organizing the Practical Christian Life

Saint Paul envisions communal life with a sense of realism. Social groups strive for a sense of unity, purpose, and cohesion. Differences and problems need to be addressed and resolved for the sake of the common good.

Practical advice is offered. The Christian community ought to be recognizably different as to how this group interacts among its own members and to those who are not. In many ways, the Christian community is countercultural and witnesses to a different set of values and lifestyle that others will notice.

1

I therefore, the prisoner in the Lord, beg you to lead a life worthy of the calling to which you have been called, with all humility and gentleness, with patience, bearing with one another in love, making every effort to maintain the unity of the Spirit in the bond of peace. (Eph 4:1–3)

2

The peace of God, which surpasses all understanding, will guard your hearts and minds in Christ Jesus. (Phil 4:7)

3
Saint Thomas

From now on, therefore, we regard no one from a human point of view; even though we once knew Christ from a human point of view, we know him no longer in that way. (2 Cor 5:16)

4

Let us then pursue what makes for peace and for mutual upbuilding. (Rom 14:19)

5

Whatever you do, in word or deed, do everything in the name of the Lord Jesus, giving thanks to God the Father through him. (Col 3:17)

6

...For we are the temple of the living God; as God said, "I will live in them and walk among them, and I will be their God, and they shall be my people." (2 Cor 6:16)

7

For we are God's servants, working together; you are God's field, God's building. (1 Cor 3:9)

8

The Lord's servant must not be quarrelsome but kindly to everyone, an apt teacher, patient, correcting opponents with gentleness... (2 Tim 2:24–25)

9

Let us therefore no longer pass judgment on one another, but resolve instead never to put a stumbling block or hindrance in the way of another. (Rom 14:13)

10

Anyone whom you forgive, I also forgive. What I have forgiven, if I have forgiven anything, has been for your sake in the presence of Christ. (2 Cor 2:10)

11

Saint Benedict

…Pursue righteousness, godliness, faith, love, endurance, gentleness. (1 Tim 6:11)

12

Beloved, never avenge yourselves, but leave room for the wrath of God; for it is written, "Vengeance is mine, I will repay, says the Lord." (Rom 12:19)

13

Examine yourselves to see whether you are living in the faith. Test yourselves. Do you not realize that Jesus Christ is in you?—unless, indeed, you fail to meet the test! (2 Cor 13:5)

14

For we hear that some of you are living in idleness, mere busybodies, not doing any work. Now such persons we command and exhort in the Lord Jesus Christ to do their work quietly and to earn their own living. (2 Thess 3:11–12)

15
Saint Bonaventure

"For the love of money is a root of all kinds of evil, and in their eagerness to be rich some have wandered away from the faith and pierced themselves with many pains." (1 Tim 6:10)

16
Our Lady of Mount Carmel

God is able to provide you with every blessing in abundance, so that by always having enough of everything, you may share abundantly in every good work. (2 Cor 9:8)

17

"In all this I have given you an example that by such work we must support the weak, remembering the words of Lord Jesus, for he himself said, 'It is more blessed to give than to receive.'" (Acts 20:35)

18
"You will be enriched in every way for your great generosity, which will produce thanksgiving to God..." (2 Cor 9:11)

19
...Teach and admonish one another in all wisdom... (Col 3:16)

20
Our hope for you is unshaken; for we know that as you share in our sufferings, so also you share in our consolation. (2 Cor 1:7)

21
"...You shall not speak evil of a leader of your people." (Acts 23:5)

22
Saint Mary Magdalene

If we are being afflicted, it is for your consolation and salvation; if we are being consoled, it is for your consolation, which you experience when you patiently endure the same sufferings that we are also suffering. (2 Cor 1:6)

23

"Come over…and help us." (Acts 16:9)

24

Since we have these promises, beloved, let us cleanse ourselves from every defilement of body and of spirit, making holiness perfect in the fear of God. (2 Cor 7:1)

25
Saint James

Keep alert, stand firm in your faith, be courageous, be strong. (1 Cor 16:13)

26
Saints Joachim and Anne, Parents of the Blessed Virgin Mary

Indeed, what once had glory has lost its glory because of the greater glory; for if what was set aside came through glory, much more has the permanent come in glory! (2 Cor 3:10–11)

27

…Let each of you lead the life that the Lord has assigned, to which God called you…(1 Cor 7:17)

28

We are afflicted in every way, but not crushed; perplexed, but not driven to despair; persecuted, but not forsaken; struck down, but not destroyed; always carrying in the body the death of Jesus, so that the life of Jesus may also be made visible in our bodies. (2 Cor 4:8–10)

29
Saint Martha

"Some even from your own group will come distorting the truth in order to entice the disciples to follow them." (Acts 20:30)

30

We have renounced the shameful things that one hides; we refuse to practice cunning or to falsify God's word; but by the open statement of the truth we commend ourselves to the conscience of everyone in the sight of God. (2 Cor 4:2)

31
Saint Ignatius of Loyola

So I do not run aimlessly, nor do I box as though beating the air; but I punish my body and enslave it, so that after proclaiming to others I myself should not be disqualified. (1 Cor 9:26–27)

August

※

The Gospel Message Requires Persistent Preaching: The Value in Writing Letters

Once accepting the gospel message and embracing the commitment that it entails, Saint Paul notes the need for a conscious and deliberate decision to act accordingly. By its very nature, the good news is meant to be shared with others. Preaching the gospel message is an ongoing work in progress.

Writing is a form of communication that requires the skills of careful thinking and clarity

Coliseum, in Ephesus, Turkey, where Saint Paul's preaching incited a riot among the local silversmiths (Acts 19:21–41)

in organization along with expression of thoughts and ideas in an understandable manner. The legacy of Saint Paul's letters in the New Testament illustrates the importance, value, and benefits of writing.

1
Saint Alphonsus Liguori

For we write you nothing other than what you can read and also understand; I hope you will understand until the end—as you have already understood us in part—that on the day of the Lord Jesus we are your boast even as you are our boast. (2 Cor 1:13–14)

2

…"I am a Jew, from Tarsus in Cilicia, a citizen of an important city; I beg you, let me speak to the people." (Acts 21:39)

3

…I had been entrusted with the gospel for the uncircumcised, just as Peter had been entrusted with the gospel for the circumcised. (Gal 2:7)

4
Saint John Mary Vianney

"When I came...to proclaim the good news of Christ, a door was opened for me in the Lord." (2 Cor 2:12)

5

See what large letters I make when I am writing in my own hand! (Gal 6:11)

6
The Transfiguration of the Lord

"...It is written in the second psalm, 'You are my Son; today I have begotten you.'" (Acts 13:33)

7

For we are not peddlers of God's word like so many; but in Christ we speak as persons of sincerity, as persons sent from God and standing in his presence. (2 Cor 2:17)

8
Saint Dominic

For the Son of God, Jesus Christ, whom we proclaimed among you…was not "Yes and No"; but in him it is always "Yes." For in him every one of God's promises is a "Yes." For this reason it is through him that we say the "Amen," to the glory of God. (2 Cor 1:19–20)

9

But thanks be to God, who in Christ always leads us in triumphal procession, and through us spreads in every place the fragrance that comes from knowing him. (2 Cor 2:14)

10
Saint Lawrence

So then, brothers and sisters, stand firm and hold fast to the traditions that you were taught by us, either by word of mouth or by our letter. (2 Thess 2:15)

11
Saint Clare

…You glorify God by your obedience to the confession of the gospel of Christ and by the generosity of your sharing with them and with all others. (2 Cor 9:13)

12

You yourselves are our letter, written on our hearts, to be known and read by all. (2 Cor 3:2)

13

We look not at what can be seen but at what cannot be seen; for what can be seen is temporary, but what cannot be seen is eternal. (2 Cor 4:18)

14
Saint Maximilian Kolbe

…"For I am ready not only to be bound but even to die in Jerusalem for the name of the Lord Jesus." (Acts 21:13)

15
The Assumption of the Blessed Virgin Mary

We know that the one who raised the Lord Jesus will raise us also with Jesus, and will bring us with you into his presence. (2 Cor 4:14)

16

You show that you are a letter of Christ, prepared by us, written not with ink but with the Spirit of the living God, not on tablets of stone but on tablets of human hearts. (2 Cor 3:3)

17

Yes, everything is for your sake, so that grace, as it extends to more and more people, may increase thanksgiving, to the glory of God. (2 Cor 4:15)

18

As we work together with him, we urge you also not to accept the grace of God in vain. (2 Cor 6:1)

19

I wrote for this reason: to test you and to know whether you are obedient in everything. (2 Cor 2:9)

20
Saint Bernard

Since it is by God's mercy that we are engaged in this ministry, we do not lose heart. (2 Cor 4:1)

21
Saint Pius X

I rejoice, because I have complete confidence in you. (2 Cor 7:16)

22
The Queenship of the Blessed Virgin Mary

For we know that if the earthly tent we live in is destroyed, we have a building from God, a house not made with hands, eternal in the heavens. (2 Cor 5:1)

23

And he died for all, so that those who live might live no longer for themselves, but for him who died and was raised for them. (2 Cor 5:15)

24
Saint Bartholomew

"I coveted no one's silver or gold or clothing. You know for yourselves that I worked with my own hands to support myself and my companions." (Acts 20:33–34)

25

And I wrote as I did, so that when I came, I might not suffer pain from those who should have made me rejoice; for I am confident about all of you, that my joy would be the joy of all of you. (2 Cor 2:3)

26

So we are always confident; even though we know that while we are at home in the body we are away from the Lord—for we walk by faith, not by sight. (2 Cor 5:6–7)

27
Saint Monica

You also join in helping us by your prayers, so that many will give thanks on our behalf for the blessing granted us through the prayers of many. (2 Cor 1:11)

28
Saint Augustine

"I did not shrink from declaring to you the whole purpose of God." (Acts 20:27)

29
The Martyrdom of Saint John the Baptist

How much more will the ministry of the Spirit come in glory? (2 Cor 3:8)

30

All this is from God, who reconciled us to himself through Christ, and has given us the ministry of reconciliation; that is, in Christ God was reconciling the world to himself, not counting their trespasses against them, and entrusting the message of reconciliation to us. (2 Cor 5:18–19)

31

So although I wrote to you, it was not on account of the one who did the wrong, nor on account of the one who was wronged, but in order that your zeal for us might be made known to you before God. (2 Cor 7:12)

September

Exhortations and Positive Thoughts for Christian Living

As both a preacher and author, Saint Paul realized the need for positive exhortations that encourage and support others. Short and concise maxims both motivate and serve as a basis for evaluating one's actions as a Christian.

Saint Paul's evocative words and images form the basis for teachings that exhibit the power of positive thinking, the challenge to improve, the goals for which to strive, and the ongoing need to do better in one's life. Such exhortations and positive thoughts are especially helpful during difficult moments in our lives.

Library, archaeological site, present-day Ephesus, Turkey

1

...Do not claim to be wiser than you are. (Rom 12:16)

2

Let each of you look not to your own interests, but to the interests of others. (Phil 2:4)

3

Saint Gregory the Great

...Do not let the sun go down on your anger. (Eph 4:26)

4

Avoid profane chatter, for it will lead people into more and more impiety. (2 Tim 2:16)

5

Bless those who persecute you; bless and do not curse them. (Rom 12:14)

6

Bear one another's burdens... (Gal 6:2)

7

In Christ Jesus, then, I have reason to boast of my work for God. (Rom 15:17)

8

The Nativity of the Blessed Virgin Mary

…Sing psalms, hymns, and spiritual songs to God. (Col 3:16)

9

Beloved, pray for us. (1 Thess 5:25)

10

…God loves a cheerful giver. (2 Cor 9:7)

11

Take the helmet of salvation, and the sword of the Spirit, which is the word of God. (Eph 6:17)

12

Do not lag in zeal, be ardent in spirit, serve the Lord. (Rom 12:11)

13

Saint John Chrysostom

Be imitators of me, as I am of Christ. (1 Cor 11:1)

14
The Exaltation of the Holy Cross

May I never boast of anything except the cross of our Lord Jesus Christ, by which the world has been crucified to me, and I to the world. (Gal 6:14)

15
Our Lady of Sorrows

Rejoice with those who rejoice, weep with those who weep. (Rom 12:15)

16

"Let the one who boasts, boast in the Lord." (2 Cor 10:17)

17

Conduct yourselves wisely toward outsiders, making the most of the time. (Col 4:5)

18

Rejoice in hope, be patient in suffering, persevere in prayer. (Rom 12:12)

19

Let us not become conceited, competing against one another, envying one another. (Gal 5:26)

20

...Extend hospitality to strangers. (Rom 12:13)

21

Saint Matthew

"Let the word of Christ dwell in you richly..." (Col 3:16)

22

Let the same mind be in you that was in Christ Jesus. (Phil 2:5)

23

Those who are taught the word must share in all good things with their teacher. (Gal 6:6)

24

If it is possible, so far as it depends on you, live peaceably with all. (Rom 12:18)

25

Live your life in a manner worthy of the gospel of Christ... (Phil 1:27)

26

"If your enemies are hungry, feed them; if they are thirsty, give them something to drink..." (Rom 12:20)

27
Saint Vincent de Paul

Brothers and sisters, do not be weary in doing what is right. (2 Thess 3:13)

28

Live in harmony with one another; do not be haughty but associate with the lowly... (Rom 12:16)

29
Saints Michael, Gabriel, and Raphael

Take no part in the unfruitful works of darkness, but instead expose them. (Eph 5:11)

30
Saint Jerome

The word of God is not chained. (2 Tim 2:9)

Hill, in Ephesus, Turkey, where
Saint Paul was imprisoned

October

The Ongoing Mission of Evangelization: Proclaiming the Good News Continues

As a missionary, Saint Paul sought creative opportunities and welcomed new ways to preach the gospel message. He saw the value of dialogue between religion and society and the intersection of faith and culture.

Feeling a sense of urgency in what was asked of him, Saint Paul was passionate in what he believed. His dedication, fidelity, and tireless and relentless efforts are exhibited in his preaching along with establishing communities in various parts of the first-century Mediterranean world of the Roman Empire.

Saint Paul was inspired by a vision and committed to a mission. We are invited to imitate his example by looking around, seeking new and creative ways to proclaim the gospel message to our contemporary age. The mission lies before us and a great deal of work still needs to be done.

1
Saint Thérèse of the Child Jesus

When I was a child, I spoke like a child, I thought like a child, I reasoned like a child; when I became an adult, I put an end to childish ways. (1 Cor 13:11)

2
The Guardian Angels

"Friends....We are mortals just like you, and we bring you good news, that you should turn from these worthless things to the living God, who made the heaven and the earth and the sea and all that is in them." (Acts 14:15)

3

For I want you to know, brothers and sisters, that the gospel that was proclaimed by me is not of human origin; for I did not receive it from a human source, nor was I taught it, but I received it through a revelation of Jesus Christ. (Gal 1:11–12)

4

Saint Francis of Assisi

As shoes for your feet put on whatever will make you ready to proclaim the gospel of peace. (Eph 6:15)

5

How are they to proclaim him unless they are sent? As it is written, "How beautiful are the feet of those who bring good news!" (Rom 10:15)

6

"Stand upright on your feet." (Acts 14:10)

7

Our Lady of the Rosary

For God, whom I serve with my spirit by announcing the gospel of his Son, is my witness that without ceasing I remember you always in my prayers. (Rom 1:9)

8

"To this day I have had help from God, and so I stand here, testifying to both small and great, saying nothing but what the prophets and Moses said would take place: that the Messiah must suffer, and that, by being the first to rise from the dead, he would proclaim light both to our people and to the Gentiles." (Acts 26:22–23)

9

Faith comes from what is heard, and what is heard comes through the word of Christ. (Rom 10:17)

10

"Believe [in] the Lord Jesus, and you will be saved, you and your household." (Acts 16:31)

11

For one believes with the heart and so is justified, and one confesses with the mouth and so is saved. (Rom 10:10)

12

To the weak I became weak, so that I might win the weak. I have become all things to all people, that I might by all means save some. I do it all for the sake of the gospel, so that I may share in its blessings. (1 Cor 9:22–23)

13

I pray that the sharing of your faith may become effective when you perceive all the good that we may do for Christ. (Phlm 1:6)

14

Of this gospel I have become a servant according to the gift of God's grace that was given me by the working of his power. (Eph 3:7)

15

Saint Teresa of Jesus

Proclaim the message; be persistent whether the time is favorable or unfavorable; convince, rebuke, and encourage, with the utmost patience in teaching. (2 Tim 4:2)

16

Let your speech always be gracious, seasoned with salt, so that you may know how you ought to answer everyone. (Col 4:6)

17
Saint Ignatius of Antioch

Be steadfast, immovable, always excelling in the work of the Lord, because you know that in the Lord your labor is not in vain. (1 Cor 15:58)

18
Saint Luke

All scripture is inspired by God and is useful for teaching, for reproof, for correction, and for training in righteousness, so that everyone who belongs to God may be proficient, equipped for every good work. (2 Tim 3:16–17)

19
Saints Isaac Jogues and John de Brébeuf

The one who sows sparingly will also reap sparingly, and the one who sows bountifully will also reap bountifully. (2 Cor 9:6)

20

So let us not grow weary in doing what is right, for we will reap at harvest time, if we do not give up. (Gal 6:9)

21

Think of us in this way, as servants of Christ and stewards of God's mysteries. (1 Cor 4:1)

22

Welcome those who are weak in faith, but not for the purpose of quarreling over opinions. (Rom 14:1)

23

"Come, let us return and visit the believers in every city where we proclaimed the word of the Lord and see how they are doing." (Acts 15:36)

24

Render service with enthusiasm, as to the Lord and not to men and women, knowing that whatever good we do, we will receive the same again from the Lord... (Eph 6:7–8)

25

"And now I commend you to God and to the message of his grace, a message that is able to build you up and to give you the inheritance among all who are sanctified." (Acts 20:32)

26

Keep on doing the things that you have learned and received and heard and seen in me, and the God of peace will be with you. (Phil 4:9)

27

Let no evil talk come out of your mouths, but only what is useful for building up, as there is no need, so that your words may give grace to those who hear. (Eph 4:29)

28

Saints Simon and Jude

"The Lord has commanded us, saying: 'I have set you to be a light for the Gentiles, so that you may bring salvation to the ends of the earth.'" (Acts 13:47)

29

I thank my God through Jesus Christ for all of you, because your faith is proclaimed throughout the world. (Rom 1:8)

30
"I did not shrink from doing anything helpful, proclaiming the message to you and teaching you publicly and from house to house." (Acts 20:20)

31
"Finally, brothers and sisters, pray for us, so that the word of the Lord may spread rapidly and be glorified everywhere, just as it is among you." (2 Thess 3:1)

Mosaic of Saint Paul, Saint Saviour in Chora, Istanbul, Turkey

November

༄

The Hope of the Resurrection: The Promise of Eternal Life

November is a month to remember and to pray for those who have died and have gone before us. Death is a reminder of our mortality and raises the ultimate questions about the meaning of human existence.

Saint Paul uses an image from his former profession of being a tentmaker to describe and explain our human existence (2 Cor 5:1–10). A tent is a temporary dwelling place. We are all sojourners and fellow travelers on the journey of faith. Moving from place to place in the various times of our lives, we meet diverse people along the way and interact with them through the eyes of faith.

The day will come when our earthly pilgrimage will end. What we experience here and now is only a foretaste and promise of something greater to come: the hope of the resurrection of the dead.

1
All Saints

I pray that you may have the power to comprehend, with all the saints, what is the breadth and length and height and depth, and to know the love of Christ that surpasses knowledge, so that you may be filled with all the fullness of God. (Eph 3:18–19)

2
The Commemoration of All the Faithful Departed (All Souls)

For if we have been united with him in a death like his, we will certainly be united with him in a resurrection like his. (Rom 6:5)

3

"I have a hope in God—a hope that they themselves also accept—that there will be a resurrection of both the righteous and the unrighteous." (Acts 24:15)

4

Saint Charles Borromeo

Blessed be the God and Father of our Lord Jesus Christ, the Father of mercies and the God of all consolation, who consoles us in all our affliction, so that we may be able to console those who are in any affliction with the consolation with which we ourselves are consoled by God. (2 Cor 1:3–4)

5

Do you not know that all of us who have been baptized into Christ Jesus were baptized into his death? (Rom 6:3)

6

Now if Christ is proclaimed as raised from the dead, how can some of you say there is no resurrection of the dead? (1 Cor 15:12)

7

I want to know Christ and the power of his resurrection and the sharing of his sufferings by becoming like him in his death, if somehow I may attain the resurrection from the dead. (Phil 3:10–11)

8

For since death came through a human being, the resurrection of the dead has also come through a human being; for as all die in Adam, so all will be made alive in Christ. (1 Cor 15:21–22)

9

The Dedication of the Lateran Basilica in Rome

In him the whole structure is joined together and grows into a holy temple in the Lord; in whom you also are built together spiritually into a dwelling place for God. (Eph 2:21–22)

10

Saint Leo the Great

If we have died with Christ, we believe that we will also live with him. (Rom 6:8)

11
Saint Martin of Tours

Our citizenship is in heaven, and it is from there that we are expecting a Savior, the Lord Jesus Christ. (Phil 3:20)

12
Saint Josaphat

Set your minds on things that are above, not on things that are on earth. (Col 3:2)

13
Saint Frances Xavier Cabrini

If we live, we live to the Lord, and if we die, we die to the Lord; so then, whether we live or whether we die, we are the Lord's. (Rom 14:8)

14

The first man was from the earth, a man of dust; the second man is from heaven. As was the man of dust, so are those who are of the dust; and as is the man of heaven, so are those who are of heaven. (1 Cor 15:47–48)

15
Saint Albert the Great

For since we believe that Jesus died and rose again, even so, through Jesus, God will bring with him those who have died. (1 Thess 4:14)

16

We have been buried with him by baptism into death, so that, just as Christ was raised from the dead by the glory of the Father, so we too might walk in the newness of life. (Rom 6:4)

17
Saint Elizabeth of Hungary

Fight the good fight of the faith; take hold of the eternal life, to which you were called... (1 Tim 6:12)

18

Then we who are alive, who are left, will be caught up in the clouds together with them to meet the Lord in the air; and so we will be with the Lord forever. Therefore encourage one another with these words. (1 Thess 4:17–18)

19

If the Spirit of him who raised Jesus from the dead dwells in you, he who raised Christ from the dead will give life to your mortal bodies also through his Spirit that dwells in you. (Rom 8:11)

20

The sting of death is sin, and the power of sin is the law. But thanks be to God, who gives us the victory through our Lord Jesus Christ. (1 Cor 15:56–57)

21

The Presentation of the Blessed Virgin Mary

For I am convinced that neither death, nor life, nor angels, nor rulers, nor things present, nor things to come, nor powers, nor height, nor depth, nor anything else in all creation, will be able to separate us from the love of God in Christ Jesus our Lord. (Rom 8:38–39)

22
Saint Cecilia

Listen, I will tell you a mystery! We will not all die, but we will all be changed, in a moment, in the twinkling of an eye, at the last trumpet. For the trumpet will sound, and the dead will be raised imperishable, and we will be changed. (1 Cor 15:51–52)

23

Why do you pass judgment on your brother or sister? Or you, why do you despise your brother or sister? For we will all stand before the judgment seat of God. So then, each of us will be accountable to God. (Rom 14:10, 12)

24
Saint Andrew Dung-Lac and Companions

Just as we have borne the image of the man of dust, we will also bear the image of the man of heaven. (1 Cor 15:49)

25

We do not live to ourselves, and we do not die to ourselves. (Rom 14:7)

26
So if you have been raised with Christ, seek the things that are above, where Christ is, seated at the right hand of God. (Col 3:1)

27
As for me, I am already being poured out as a libation, and the time of my departure has come. I have fought the good fight, I have finished the race, I have kept the faith. (2 Tim 4:6–7)

28
"I do not count my life of any value to myself, if only I may finish my course and the ministry that I received from the Lord Jesus, to testify to the good news of God's grace." (Acts 20:24)

29
The last enemy to be destroyed is death. (1 Cor 15:26)

30
Saint Andrew

I press on toward the goal for the prize of the heavenly call of God in Christ Jesus. (Phil 3:14)

Present-day archaeological site of Derbe, Turkey
(Acts 14:20)

100 ❧ *Saint Paul the Apostle for Every Day*

December

Recalling the First Coming of Jesus in History: Preparing for Christ's Return in Majesty

The liturgical season of Advent is a time to recall three important moments in time in which the Lord Jesus comes to humanity: the past (history), the present (mystery), and the future (majesty).

Saint Paul was well aware about the importance of time and stressed the need to make good use of the time that is available to us. Recalling the past enables us to live in the present moment along with a sense of hope and anticipation for the days that lie ahead.

As the winter season approaches with its dark days, we are invited to remember that the true light has already come into the world, to continue to live in the light of faith, and to prepare the world for that future day until the Lord Jesus will return in his glory.

1

Grace to you and peace from God our Father and the Lord Jesus Christ, who gave himself for our sins to set us free from the present evil age, according to the will of our God and Father, to whom be the glory forever and ever. Amen. (Gal 1:3–5)

2

...See, now is the acceptable time; see, now is the day of salvation! (2 Cor 6:2)

3

Saint Francis Xavier

Rejoice always, pray without ceasing, give thanks in all circumstances; for this is the will of God in Christ Jesus for you. (1 Thess 5:16–18)

4

Rejoice in the Lord always; again I will say, Rejoice. (Phil 4:4)

5

...I charge you to keep the commandment without spot or blame until the manifestation of our Lord Jesus Christ, which he will bring about at the right time—he who is the blessed and only Sovereign, the King of kings and Lord of lords. (1 Tim 6:13–15)

6
Saint Nicholas

Do not worry about anything, but in everything by prayer and supplication with thanksgiving let you your requests be made known to God. (Phil 4:6)

7
Saint Ambrose

Do not be conformed to this world, but be transformed by the renewing of your minds, so that you may discern what is the will of God—what is good and acceptable and perfect. (Rom 12:2)

8
The Immaculate Conception of the Blessed Virgin Mary

Consider your own call, brothers and sisters; not many of you were wise by human standards, not many were powerful, not many were of noble birth. But God chose what is foolish in the world to shame the wise; God chose what is weak in the world to shame the strong. (1 Cor 1:26–27)

9

For it is the God who said, "Let light shine out of darkness," who has shone in our hearts to give the light of the knowledge of the glory of God in the face of Jesus Christ. (2 Cor 4:6)

10

For you are all children of light and children of the day; we are not of the night or of darkness. (1 Thess 5:5)

11

For all of us must appear before the judgment seat of Christ, so that each may receive recompense for what has been done... (2 Cor 5:10)

12
Our Lady of Guadalupe

Be careful then how you live, not as unwise people but as wise, making the most of the time... (Eph 5:15–16)

13
Saint Lucy

Look at what is before your eyes... (2 Cor 10:7)

14
Saint John of the Cross

May the God of peace himself sanctify you entirely; and may your spirit and soul and body be kept sound and blameless at the coming of our Lord Jesus Christ. (1 Thess 5:23)

15

I consider that the sufferings of this present time are not worth comparing with the glory about to be revealed to us. (Rom 8:18)

16

For you know the generous act of our Lord Jesus Christ, that though he was rich, yet for your sakes he became poor, so that by his poverty you might become rich. (2 Cor 8:9)

17
"As John was finishing his work, he said, 'What do you suppose that I am? I am not he. No, but one is coming after me; I am not worthy to untie the thong of the sandals on his feet.'" (Acts 13:25)

18
If we hope for what we do not see, we wait for it with patience. (Rom 8:25)

19
So then let us not fall asleep as others do, but let us keep awake and be sober. (1 Thess 5:6)

20
"You descendants of Abraham's family, and others who fear God, to us the message of this salvation has been sent." (Acts 13:26)

21
You, beloved, are not in darkness, for that day to surprise you like a thief. (1 Thess 5:4)

22

From now on there is reserved for me the crown of righteousness, which the Lord, the righteous judge, will give me on that day, and not only to me but also to all who have longed for his appearing. (2 Tim 4:8)

23

Let your gentleness be known to everyone. The Lord is near. (Phil 4:5)

24

...For salvation is nearer to us now than when we became believers; the night is far gone, the day is near. Let us then lay aside the works of darkness and put on the armor of light. (Rom 13:11–12)

25

The Nativity of the Lord

For the grace of God has appeared, bringing salvation to all. (Titus 2:11)

26
Saint Stephen

"And while the blood of your witness Stephen was shed, I myself was standing by, approving and keeping the coats of those who killed him." (Acts 22:20)

27
Saint John

For once you were darkness, but now in the Lord you are light. Live as children of light. (Eph 5:8)

28
The Holy Innocents

..."It is through many persecutions that we must enter the kingdom of God." (Acts 14:22)

29

To the King of the ages, immortal, invisible, the only God, be honor and glory forever and ever. Amen. (1 Tim 1:17)

30
May he so strengthen your hearts in holiness that you may be blameless before our God and Father at the coming of our Lord Jesus with all his saints. (1 Thess 3:13)

31
I am confident of this, that the one who began a good work among you will bring it to completion by the day of Jesus Christ. (Phil 1:6)